1960 1961 1962 1963 1964 1965 1966

N THE 1960s, the young people of the country sought to extend their personal freedoms, much to the chagrin of parents and grandparents, most of whom could readily recall the shortages and hardships of the immediate post war era, only some 15 years before.

However, the teenagers were not to be denied and even in Arbroath the trend towards 'flower power' and discafes seemed unstoppable. Coke and Fanta were the 'in' drinks for those too young to sample something stronger and premises which provided a haven for both sexes from father's intransigence and mother's nagging flourished.

The town came out of the doldrums with industry busier than ever and the fishing fleet beginning to modernise after years of austerity. New housing was essential for the development of the town and both municipal and private schemes sprouted. Sadly, in some eyes, the characterful 'prefabs' which had provided low-cost housing after the Second World War were lost in the process.

Similarly, a lot of perfectly good houses between Ladyloan and Millgate Loan and in the town centre paid the price of 'progress' when the bulldozers moved in and they were cleared to make way for Arbroath's new Inner Relief Road'.

With the new houses and an influx of people came a need for new schools and this was met with the opening of a brand new facility, Arbroath Academy, in the north of the burgh.

Motor cars were the personal possession that everyone craved and more and more were to be seen as factories modernised both their equipment and their product to cater for increased demand.

Every teenager's dream was to own his or her own Mini, that immortal flight of fancy in pressed steel designed by the creative genius of Alex Issigonis. And Scotland, too, had its own car industry, with the Hillman Imp being manufactured by Rootes at Linwood, near Edinburgh.

Fashion statements, made initially in London, worked their way north and winklepickers and skin tight trousers were de rigeur and uncomfortable at the same time. Mods on their Vespas and Lambrettas paraded through the town and along King's Drive and, for a while, a gang culture prevailed in Arbroath.

The Sharks, made up of local 'Rockers', met in the Squirrel Cafe, Kirk Square, and the Mods were generally to be found in the Discafe in Commerce Street. 'Fishy Fleet', as the name suggests was made up of young men from the Fit o' the Toon and they had a roving commission.

On the sporting front, Arbroath FC continued to fly the flag and, for those of a gentler persuasion, the vagaries of the Scottish weather were dispensed with when Arbroath Indoor Bowling Stadium was opened by Arbroath's own Andy Stewart.

On the political front, Members of the European Parliament and Members of the Scottish Parliament were still years away, the

Arbr
Sout
Dun
wher
Gard   Conservative.

In 1968, the Scottish National Party put forward candidates at the Town Council elections for the first time, with all four being elected. A sign of things to come!

Brian J. Forsyth

Front cover - For many years, Arbroath was the venue for the Angus Show, the annual extravaganza of all things agricultural in the county. Our picture shows a large crowd on the Braeheids at Victoria Park and round the arena watching a show-jumping competition from the 1967 show.

Back cover - One of the main attractions of Arbroath as a holiday resort both before the Second World War and after, until the advent of cheap jet travel made package holidays in sunnier climes attractive, was the impressive Outdoor Bathing Pool at Queen's Drive. Our picture shows an uncharacteristicaly quiet pool on a beautiful summer day in 1963.

Wir Bookie o' the 1960s, by Brian J. Forsyth. Published by Johnston (Falkirk) Ltd., Redbrae Road, Camelon, Falkirk, FK1 4ZA. November, 2005

The generosity of Dundee art collector, Mr James Proctor Norwell, in January, 1960, saw eight works by James Watterston Herald donated to the Arbroath collection. They included watercolours and pastel drawings from various stages of his career. Our picture shows the presentation ceremony in the Public Library attended by, from left - Mr Norman Crawford, librarian; Mr William L. Reid, chairman of the library committee; Mrs John Matthew, convener of the art committee; Mr Norwell, Mr Ernest F. Cobb, former chairman of the library committee; and Mrs James Norwell, jnr, who handed over the gift.

Wives of the King from Arbroath Amateur Operatic Society's presentation of 'The King and I' in the Webster Theatre in February, 1960. They are, from left, back row - Ala Rodger, Jessica Hogg, Margaret Hutchinson and June Stockham: middle row - Eliza Suttie, Marlene Hayward, Norma Hamilton and Joan Mitchell: front row - Pat Jamieson, Marlene Kear, Evelyn Robertson, Ruth Gordon and Evelyn Malcolm.

After being closed for five months for major renovations and restoration, Abbey Parish Church reopened on Sunday, March 20, 1960, when the Rev. Dr Harry C. Whitley, St Giles Cathedral, Edinburgh, officiated at the morning service, assisted by the Rev Archibald Russell, minister of the church. Pictured on that occasion are officiating clergy and elders and officials of the congregation. They are, from left, back row - R. Lawson, G.C. Baird, J. Morrison, A. Wilson, D. Wyllie, F. Wyllie, J. Cant and E. Meekison: middle row - Norman Low, R. Innes, H. Crichton, W. Martin, Dr Whitley, Mr Russell, S. Dilly, organist; A. Lowson, H. Mair, D.D. Wilson and Theo Ross: front row - Campbell Robertson, K. Cameron, D. Lowden, Peter Graham, E.W.R. Myles, D.W. McFarlane, J. Fraser, A. Shepherd, T. Paton and D. Gove.

Admiral J.H.F. Crombie, a former Flag Officer (Scotland) performed the opening ceremony of the new Royal Naval Association premises in Panmure Street in March, 1960. On his arrival, he was piped aboard by three members of the Association. In the main group are, from left - Captain G.W. Tanner, commanding officer of HMS Condor; Admiral Crombie, Commander T.C.A.H. Ouchterloney, The Guynd; Joe Riley, chairman; and Provost D.A. Gardner.

In 1960, Alloa Breweries sought unusual locations to site a promotional campaign and one of the places chosen was the local yard of Gerrard Bros., Boatbuilders, where our picture was taken. The Alloa company picked the occasion of the launch of the fishing vessel, 'Endeavour', skippered by John Swankie, for their visit and provided refreshments from the nearby Gayfield Bar. Cheerfully proposing a collective toast with their free bottles of Calder's Ale are, from left, back row - Jim Brown, Drew Crichton, Bob Mackay, Bob Strachan, Bob Smith, Merry Coull and Ivor Davidson: middle row - Charlie Grant, Ron McDonald, Bobby Dunn, --------, Andy Coull, Joe Law and Clem Jolly: front row - John Duthie, Alloa Brewery; Peter 'Pro' Robertson, Dorwards Bar; -------- and --------.

This scene depicts the top of James Street as it was in 1960. The ground floor of the two story central block, 3/5 James Street, at one time housed 'Pop Allan's' pawnbroker's shop above which was housing. At the corner was the shop of W.B. Williamson, baker. The entire corner complex is now occupied by Swinton Insurance. Round the corner, on High Street, were Ruxton's butcher shop; Davidson's Sweetie Shop and Fit-Rite, outfitter. The Ford Zodiac in the foreground was owned by Mr George Ruxton, and the 13 cwt Fordson van was originally bought by Mr Alex W. Hunter, Arbroath, and in the picture is lettered as owned by Williamson the baker. The public convenience adjacent to the Don Jon Tower, the entrance to which can be clearly seen, was well known during the summer months for the particularly nasty odour which permeated the entire area, and was eventually bricked up.

Pupils from Inverbrothock Primary School who were placed second equal in the Recorder Bands (Primary Schools) class at Arbroath and District Musical Festival in the Webster Theatre in May, 1960. They are, from left, back - Kathleen Wallace, Violet McLean, Janice Boath, Patricia Daniels and Patricia Wood: front - Yvonne Smith, ---- Wyllie, Helen Smith, Mary Nicoll and Jane Daniels.

The 7th Arbroath (St Andrew's Church) Company, Boys' Brigade, in the church hall in 1960. Pictured are, from left, back row - S. Laing, R. Milne, A. Hosie, J. Smith, Lieutenant Earl Matthew, G. Christie, B. Webster, -------- and S. Foster: middle row - David Gerrard, K. Falconer, --------, -------, M. Coutts, G. Reaney, C. Mathers, D. Foster and M. Beattie: front row - Beatrice Gerrard, N. Beattie, E. Huggins, B. Mason, D. Matthew, J. Hutcheson, C. Wren and J. Greenhowe.

This charming picture was taken from the top of Signal Tower during the summer of 1960 and shows the bustling community which existed at that time between Millgate Loan and Ladyloan. The group of buildings at the right foreground famously contained Greg Mandla's chip shop, before the business was moved across the road following the decimation of the area for the 'inner relief road'. In the centre of the picture is the corner of Glover Street and Ladyloan, with the corner shop run by John and Agnes Stephenson. A few doors along, at 53 Ladyloan is a similar establishment owned at the time by Mrs J. Fairweather and purchased some three years later by George Vettese.

A blast from the past! The cocktail bar at the Cliffburn Hotel as it was in 1960. Access was gained off the corridor beyond reception or from the ground floor dining area through the door to the left of the picture.

This happy group was pictured in 1960. Those present are, from left - Robert McGlashan, David Goodwillie, Provost J.K. Moir, Frank Thornton (just visible behind the Provost), R.R. Spink, Alex Keith, Adam Cargill, John Eddie, John Duff, David Smith and William Smith. The odd man out in the group of Arbroath Town Council elected members and officials is the recipient of the television, John Eddie, who with his brother ran a watchmaker's and jeweller's business at 90 High Street. Mr Eddie maintained and wound the town's clocks for many years, and the television was presented to him on his retiral.

This group is taken from the archives of the 2nd Arbroath Scouts and shows members of Pheasant Patrol at summer camp at Haughend, Glenesk, in July, 1960. Pictured with their neatly laid out kit are, from left - Eric Cronshaw, Neil Smith, Denis Smart, Ian Manders, Ray Will and John Swankie.

Arbroath special constables of Angus Constabulary who were presented with long-service awards in November, 1960. They are, from left, back - Stan L. Laing, David Boath, John S. Mentiply, --------, William McKenzie, James Cant, Norman Riddle, Peter Cowie, D.Y. Walker and William J. Hutton: front - Frank Conacher, the Rev. Archie Russell, --------, George A. Jervie, Alex J.B. Hogg, Pat M. Hayes and --------.

Page 13

Members of Miss Gordon's Ladies' Choir at their second annual concert held in the Webster Theatre in December, 1960. Their guest artist was Mr Peter Glossop, baritone. Pictured are, from left, back row - Joyce Matthew, Jeanette Geddes, --------, Margaret Fotheringham, Sandra Maxwell, Pat McFarlane, Catriona Moffat, Mary Talbert, Morag Pert, Sandra Anderson and Jean Addison: middle row - Anna Pert, Rita Farmer, Constance Grossett, Peggy Grieve, Betty Crowe, Lily Mathieson, Sheena Crouch, Morag Campbell, Aileen Campbell, Muriel Thompson and Dorothy Furye: front row - Maureen Philip, Doris Mathieson, Robert Forbes, choir accompanist; Elizabeth Gordon, conductor; Mr Glossop, Annie Doig Winter, soloist's accompanist; Sandra Shepherd and Isabel Morrison.

This picture carries us back to when the industrial heartland of Arbroath - along the valley of the Brothock Burn - bustled with activity. The year was 1961 and many of the buildings in our picture disappeared shortly after. In the centre foreground, the imposing ruin of Arbroath Abbey is instantly recognisable, with the Abbot's House to the left and the Abbey burial ground to the right. Across the road, in Hamilton Green, at the partly demolished junction, is the Red Lion public house. The new high-rise buildings at extreme right are at Smithy Croft and the bottom of Grant Road. The street leading into the distance at the right is Guthrie Port, with the remnants of The Wyndies between it and the new flats. The road is carried over the railway, past the huge Giddings & Lewis-Fraser, Ltd., industrial complex on the left, by the High Road Bridge and becomes Cairnie Street. The large building at the junction of Cairnie Street and Lochlands Street, at Stobcross, was also part of the Giddings & Lewis-Fraser manufacturing plant. Down from the Abbey, the thoroughfare is James Street, with the Palace Cinema on the left and Inverbrothock Parish Church at the junction on the right. Over the road in Arrott Street, the low building with the dormer windows is the Sea Cadet Hall. Continuing towards the top of the picture is the building which housed the Tunnel Bar, in Robert Street, and further on still is the sclatter of houses in St Mary Street, Green Street, Rossie Street, Russell Street, Fergus Street, etc. The large building left of centre was the locomotive shed at the railway goods depot and at the top, just visible, is Arbroath High School and the line of trees is Keptie Widdie. The field at top right is the site of the new Arbroath High School. The open area at top centre is Macdonald Park, with Lochlands Bowling Club's green visible.

The Rev. Gavin D. (Guy) Brownlie was inducted to the charge of Ladyloan Church on Friday, March 5, 1961. He succeeded the Rev. John E. Pool. The service was conducted by the Rev. T. Gemmell Campbell, Old Church, Moderator of Arbroath Presbytery, and the charges were given by the Rev. Ian MacEwan, Inverkeilor and Lunan Church. Addresses were given by the ministers present and Mr Brownlie received a number of presentations. On the Sunday following the induction, Mr Brownlie was introduced at the morning service by his father-in-law. the Rev. George N. Duff, Albert Drive Church, Glasgow. In our picture, taken following the induction service, are, from left - Rev. George Duff; Jim McLeod, Presbytery Elder, Ladyloan Church; Rev. Frank Clark, Carnoustie St Stephen's; Rev. Alastair Dykes and Rev. Murray Leishman, friends of Mr Brownlie; Rev. George Gillon, Barry, Presbytery Clerk; Rev. T. Gemmell Campbell; Rev. Brownlie; Rev. Ian MacEwan; Mr Tom Lyon, Elder, Knox's Church; Rev. John Reid, Knox's Church; Rev. Archibald Russell, Abbey Church; Rev. Ian MacLeod, St Andrew's Church; and Rev. James Hood, a friend of Mr Brownlie.

Office-bearers of the Arbroath branch of the British Legion pictured at the annual 'bully beef' night in the Helen Street clubrooms in March, 1961. They are, from left - Mr Charles Kinnear, secretary; Mr A. Cargill, treasurer; Mr N. Barron, Montrose; Brigadier James A. Oliver, Colonel George W. Dunn, chairman; Councillor David Goodwillie, area vice-chairman; and Mr Tom Matheson, national chairman.

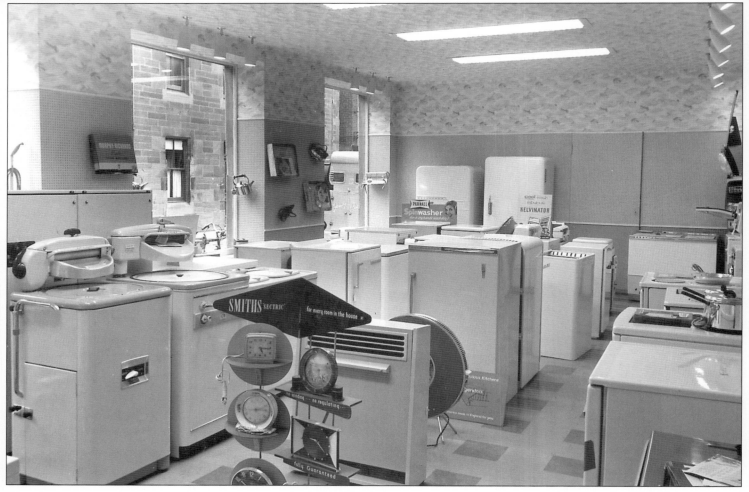

The design of kitchen appliances has moved on since these 'cutting edge' white goods were photographed in the premises of Reekie at 3-5 James Street in March, 1961.

Primary seven pupils at Arbroath High School during the 1960/61 session. They are, from left, back row - John Cameron, Peter Thornton, Ross Ruxton, Angus Anderson, Russell Davidson, Eric Cronshaw, Gayre Christie, Patrick W. Anderson, James A. Cargill, David Nieve and Rowland McLean: middle row - David Kane, Ian Snowdon, Michael Powalski, Neil Ferrier, Joyce Groves, Helen Bowman, Susan Haddow, Jennifer Hunter, Priscilla Lawrie, Brian Maitland, James Cargill, Allan Jarret and John Thornton: front row - Isobel Gardener, Susan Davidson, Mary Bowman, Ann Page, Pam Sievwright, Caris Leslie, Kathleen Setton, Ann Morton, Eunice Smith, Lillian Gove, Mary Chapel, Margaret McKechnie and Jacqueline Low.

Classes 2T1 and 2D1 at Arbroath High School in 1961. Many of those pictured transferred to Arbroath Academy when it opened and formed the new school's senior year. The pupils are, from left, back row - Robert Bodman, David Beattie, Tom Grant, Wilson Eddie, Harry Hudson, George Smith, Rob Knight and Dennis Leadingham: second row - Alex Cargill, Tom McIvor, Jim McEwan, Tom Cargill, John McLeod, Brian Findlay, Robert Duncan, James Pearson and Raymond Ritchie: third row - James McCormack, Helen Robb, Norma Gordon, Gladys Williamson, Kathleen Harrison, Caroline Campbell, Patricia Rossler, Joyce Gibb, Freda Jarret and Raymond Gallagher: front row - Hilda Scott, Evelyn Bogue, Carol Hadden, Irene McKenzie, Heather Gordon, Norma Wyllie, Anne Morrison and Eileen Craig.

Page 20

Boys of form IV at Arbroath High School in 1961. They are, from left, back row - Neil Ferrier, Peter Thornton, Fred Leslie, Harold Dickson, Ian Baird, Edward McLaren, David Crawford, Dougie Robb, David Reid, Fergus Ellen, Ian Snowden and Peter Cooper: second row - Jim Waddell, Eric Cronshaw, ----------, John Steven, John Cameron, Brian Whammond, ---------- and Ian McGowan: third row - Colin Duguid, Alan Whiteside, ----------, Peter Paterson, Bob Davies, Brian Robertson, ----------, Brian Hosie, David Leadingham, Howard Evans and ---- Ross: fourth row - Murray Scott, Neil Shepherd, Duncan Ferguson, Keith Swankie, Tommy ------, Richard Jaworski, Bill Craig, Norman Cunningham, Ian Sievwright, John Thomson and Brian Dewar: front row - ----------, Ian Graham, Ian Lefevre, John Thornton, Norman Tilley and Alex Beattie.

A new air service from 'Dundee' to London was inaugurated at HMS Condor on Thursday, June 1, 1961, when a 36-seater Dan-Air Douglas Dakota left from 'Dundee's' new airport. The Admiralty had given Dan Air Services Ltd the use of accommodation at the former FORA headquarters at Ashbrooke House, Condor. Our picture shows crew members and passengers just before take-off. Recognised among the latter are Arbroath veterinarian, Mr A. Linton Robertson, local MP, Sir James Duncan, Mr John McGregor and Mr Douglas Lowe.

This bevy of local beauties worked at various factories in Arbroath but all played football as the Baffeez Bombshells, as several worked for Douglas Fraser and Sons Ltd at their Wellgate works where Baffeez - rope soled canvas shoes - were manufactured. They are pictured at Gayfield Park in 1961 prior to the final of an inter-factory ladies' tournament organised by Jim Alexander. The match was won by the team from Keith Blackman Ltd. The Bombshells are wearing Arbroath Lads' Club strips borrowed for the occasion. The trophy was presented to the winning team by Patrick O'Hagan, a popular Irish singer who was appearing at the Webster Hall at the time. The girls are, from left, back - Myra Low, Georgina Thomson, Peggy Nicoll, Dorothy Thomson, Dorothy Coull and Sandra Laing: front - Helen Laing, Sheena Guthrie, Margaret Reid, Iona Graham and Sylvia Spurway.

Originally, Fisheracre was occupied by a row of cottages, "on land belonging to the person responsible for supplying adequate food to the Abbey during Lent" according to Lawrence Burness's book 'The Streets of Arbroath Past and Present'. The cottages were demolished and in 1960 the above row of modern shops was built, our picture dating from a year later. Taylor's was a traditional grocery/sweetie shop which sold a great variety of items - a 'corner shop' that wasn't on a corner! Grimmond and Russell, butchers, were famed for their meat products, in particular sausages and mince. Arbroath Flower Centre was run by Jim and Bill McGugan and began as a garden shop, expanding into fruit and tropical fish. Many readers will remember the end of week banana sale, with fantastic bargains. The shop next door is shown with items of furniture in the windows, as it was at that time unsold and was being used as a store. It later became a Mace grocery and was bought in 1963 by Mr Percy Watt. Millar's haberdashery stocked an extensive range of hardware. The modern, full length windows with which the shops were originally equipped were largely replaced over the years by smaller ones, as owners counted the cost of vandal attacks.

A view of the ground floor lounge of the Royal Hotel, High Street, in the summer of 1961. The picture was taken from the doorway looking towards the rear of the building. Note the 'Royal' coronets engraved on the glass partitions.

An enterprising local trio set a world record in 1961 when they pushed and pulled an upright piano from Dundee to Arbroath, via Broughty Ferry, Monifieth and Carnoustie. Their feat was organised in conjunction with a successful attempt on the world record for non-stop piano playing set in the Red Triangle Hall, behind Hill Street, by 'Syncopating' Sandy Strickland. His amazing endurance feat of 133 hours beat the previous best of 132 hours set by a German musician, Heinz Antz. Our picture shows the piano pushers and pullers, from left - John Evans, David Kane and Ian Graham, being waved through Barry Village en-route. The event in the Red Triangle Hall attracted huge attention and at one stage extra police had to be called in to control the crowd of people desperate to get a close up view of 'Syncopating' Sandy's world record attempt.

Her Majesty Queen Elizabeth The Queen Mother signs the visitor's book at the Town House with a flourish during her visit to Arbroath in September, 1961, when she opened the Queen Mother Maternity Wing at Arbroath Infirmary. Looking on are, from left - Mr W.D. Smith, town clerk; Provost D.A. Gardner and Mr William Fairweather, town officer. She also attended the dedication service of the extended and refurbished St Christopher's Church at Condor.

Santa has always proved a popular visitor at Christmas parties although the young lady on his knee at this Carmyllie East Primary School primary one and two seasonal celebration of 1961 seems not too sure at being separated from mum. However, the village bobby was on hand to see that everyone had a grand time! Pictured are, from left, back - Wilma Crichton, Marilyn Rodgers, Ann McSheffery, Linda Cadger, Derek Cadger, Eleanor Whitton, James Petrie, Jill Dey, Margaret McSheffery, Anne Smith, Frances Smart, Margaret Reeves and Ann Dey: front - Patricia Paul, Muriel Birse, James Rodgers, Nancy Fechlie, Colin Buist, Alan Cadger, Audrey Duell, Philip Turner, Amy Dey and Carol Buist.

Throughout the 1960s, the YMCA Hall, Hill Street, reverberated to the sounds of local pop group, Danny and the Demonstrators driving the youngsters wild at the weekly dance. Our picture, from 1962, recalls the early days of pop when groups such as The Beatles, The Rolling Stones, The Kinks and many more were emerging to the plaudits of a new young generation. The Danny of the group's name is Danny Powell (centre), vocalist supreme who still lives in the town and works in the building trade. The others are, from left, Terry Wood, proprietor of Abbey Music, Kirk Square; Neil Campbell, who runs his own electrical contractor business in Broughty Ferry; Bill Spurway, who is similarly employed in Arbroath; and Dave Patterson, who is still living locally. The lads got together in about 1960 and their early engagements were at the Portcullis. However, their fame spread and they were soon entertaining crowds at dances in the YM Hall, the Sea Cadet Hall and later the Marine before being booked to major venues such as the JM Ballroom, where they were resident for a time, and the Palais, both Dundee, and the City Hall Perth. The group's talents were recognised by EMI who invited them to London to cut a record but, after lengthy deliberations, the lads declined the offer as most of them were in the middle of apprenticeships and they realised how risky the venture would be.

This group of scrubbed and gleaming ten-year-olds comprised members of Miss Elizabeth Gordon's Boys' Choir who had just presented a concert in Inverbrothock Church, now the Baptist Centre, James Street, in 1962. The picture was taken on the stairs leading to the balcony. Pictured are, from left, back row - Brian Pankhurst, William Scollay, Ian Yule and Derek Syme: second row - Alasdair McNaughton, David Stewart, Richard Bishop and Kenneth Birse: third row - ---- Robertson, Alan Yule and Willie Cargill: fourth row - Miss Gordon, James Dear, Sandy Singers and John Verth: front row - Neil Clark, Sandy Yule, Alistair Dutch and James Hutcheson.

Ladies of the chorus of Arbroath Amateur Operatic Society's production of 'Carousel' in the Webster Hall in 1962. They are, from left, back row - Isabel Matthews, Marion Farquhar, Grace Allan, Sheila Pert and Isobel Scott: middle row - Joan Vale, Evelyn Robertson, June Stockham, Joan Mitchell, Evelyn Malcolm and S. Fraser: front row - Marlene Findlay, Muriel Robertson, Ruth Gordon, Elaine Seroczynska, Gail McFarlane, Edna Nicoll, Sheila Scott and Mary Carini.

Pupils of the Appolinari Dance Studio and guests at their annual display in the Webster Theatre in 1962. They are, from left, back row - Nan McLeod, Conway Stuart, Rosa Appolinari, Helen Young, Pamela Johnston, Hazel Pearson, Marianne Edwards, Linda Croall, Margaret Hainsworth, Yvonne Smith, Eleanor Anderson, Aileen Grant, Sheonagh Woodhams, Colin Smith, Edwina Gillespie, George S. Shepherd and Ruby Melvin: middle row - Susan Keen, --------, Alison Mann, Marilyn Wilson, Susan Anderson, Anne Verth, Carla Doig, Cynthia Biesok, Christine Biesok, Margaret Smart, Anne Christie and Lesley Pert: front row - --------, --------, Glynis Rowlands, Mary Mylles, --------, Catherine Bell, Anne Bell, Lynne Hall, --------, Loris Cargill, Irene Martin and Lesley Nicoll.

A valuable record of the activities of the Arbroath branch of the British Legion Scotland was presented to Arbroath Public Library in March, 1962. Five large volumes comprising a scrapbook of press cuttings, photographs, programmes, etc., had been prepared by Mrs James Riley, branch archivist, covering the period from the founding of the branch in 1935 to November, 1960. Pictured at the handover in the Arbroath Room at the library are, from left - Mr Tom Matheson, national chairman of the British Legion Scotland; Mr Alex Cargill, branch vice-chairman; Mr Norman Crawford, librarian; Colonel G.W. Dunn, branch chairman; Brigadier James A. Oliver, branch president; Councillor Frank Thornton, a member of the library committee; Mr Riley and Mr Ernest F. Cobb.

Employees of D.T. Wilson and Sons Ltd, house furnishers and removers, 99 High Street, pictured during the move of Clerk, Oliver, Dewar and Webster, SSC, from their premises in Brothockbank House to the new facility on Brothock Bridge in June, 1962. Pictured are, from left - Angus Stewart, --- Ramsay, Bob Webster, Alec Anderson, David Hudson, Bill McMillan, Angus Collins and Bob Eaton.

Prizegiving at St Vigeans Primary School in June, 1962. Our picture shows Mrs Nancy Webster, Magungie, presenting the Dux Medal to David M. Gibb. The youngster with the cup is Jim Swankie. Looking on are, from left, back - David Doig, Arthur Whitton, Alice Mary Anderson, Sheona Jarret, --------, Kathleen Clark, Maureen Doig, Robert Beattie, Lizzie Longmuir, Nora Laing, Ina Binnie, Douglas Gibb, Susan Bracken, Alex Anderson, James Gibb, --------, Marjory Binnie, Brian Robb and --------: middle - Deborah Bracken, Dave Reid, Marjory Anderson, Michael Forsyth, Billy Hardie and Barbara Binnie.

Above - Arbroath Academy was opened with due pomp and circumstance on June 15, 1962. Gathering guests were greeted with 'Land of Hope and Glory' and 'Gaudeamus'. Among the many guests were Sir James A.L. Duncan, M.P., for South Angus; Provost D.A. Gardner, and other civic chiefs; Mr John Eddie, County Director of Education and Mr J.B. Yates, County Architect, who designed the school. The school was declared open by Sir William F. Arbuckle, secretary, Scottish Education Department, who was accompanied at the ceremony by Lady Arbuckle. Pictured are, from left - Lady Arbuckle, Sir William Arbuckle, Colonel William Scott, Provost D.A. Gardner, Mrs Scott, Sir James Duncan, MP; Mrs Crawford, Mr A.M. Crawford, head teacher; Mr John Eadie, Lady Duncan and the Rev Ian McLeod. Right - William Miller, a senior pupil, presented Sir William Arbuckle with a 'History of Arbroath' and Pamela Smith (extreme left) presented a bouquet to Lady Arbuckle. Looking on are Mr A.M. Crawford, headmaster; and Lieutenant-Colonel William Scott, chairman of Angus Education Committee, who presided at the ceremony.

Arbroath High School medallists from June, 1962. They are, from left, back - David J. Leadingham, technical prize; Robert G. Clark, mathematics and science prizes; Alfred C. Shedden, German prize; John W. Thornton, history prize; and Alex King, geography prize: front - Anne M. Nicoll, primary Dux; Gail M.A. Harvey, French prize; Jean F. Watt, English, Latin and Greek prizes and Dux Medal; Judith Mordecai, music prize; Wilma M.D. Cameron, homecraft prize; and Elizabeth P. Shanks, commercial prize.

Girls of Class 3A/1 at Arbroath Academy in 1962, the year the school opened. Pictured are, from left, back - Sandra Vettese, Catherine Swankie, Anne Pert, Pauline Jack, Marlyn Lindsay and Helen Burza: middle row - Jeanette Simpson, Carol Purcell, Aileen Rose, Sheila Knowles, Irene Fairweather and Phyllis Hailwood: front row - Ann Rose, June Davidson, Lena Hadden, Grace Moseley, Kay Cruickshank, Marilyn Nicoll and Frances Murray.

The Golden Lion Garage, Montrose Road, as it appeared in 1962. At that time the business was owned by Edmond Laskowski, who also had the Red Lion Garage. Visible in the picture are some of the cars of the day including a Jaguar Mark 2, a couple of Standards, a Vauxhall Cresta, a couple of Bedford vans, a Ford Zephyr, a Vauxhall Victor and a Jaguar mark 9 or 10.

This group of local men gathered in Arbirlot Church hall in October, 1962, for the inaugural meeting of Arbirlot Men's Club. Pictured are, from left, back row - Jim Traill, George Michie, Allan Swankie, Dave Guthrie, Jim Milne, Chae Hampton, Bill Ramsay, Ed Johnston and John Fullerton: middle row - John Dewars, George Walker, George Cooper, Allan Fletcher, Chae Jorgensen, Dave Fullerton, Theo Henderson, George Howe and Bill Duguid: front row - Angus McPherson, Peter Beange, Jim Fairweather, John Bell, Jock Ramsay, Dave Gibb, Peem Martin, Dave Swankie and Jim Simpson.

The junior choir of St Columba's Church gave the first of two performances of the operetta 'Dulcinetta' in the church hall at the beginning of November, 1962. Our picture shows the leading players who are, from left, back - Christine Robertson, Michelle Craig, Isobel Low, Mary Lawson, Marjory Cant and Jean Petrie: front - James Robertson, Linda Storr, Catriona McMillan, Patricia Gillespie, Sheila Graham, Kenneth McKenzie, Aileen Petrie and Ian Begg.

A bitterly cold spell during the first week of January, 1963, restricted the space available to the growing colony of swans, ducks and other waterfowl at Keptie Pond. For a time, they had only the space shown and were dependent on the generosity of nearby residents for their food. Some, however, such as the youngster in the foreground, found feeding the ducks no imposition whatsoever!

Trustees and members of the management committee of Arbroath Savings Bank at the annual general meeting in January, 1963. They are, from left, back - Alistair Fairweather, A.J.B. Hogg, George Jervie, W. Calder, Hugh Fraser, Bailie Robert R. Spink and Hugh Nelson: front - G. Lyall Manson, D. Gunn, W. Macdonald, J.H. Leuchars, chairman; ex-Provost John F. Webster, Tom King, actuary; and J. Braid.

The Gibson Memorial Fountain, a feature of Brothock Bridge for almost 100 years, was removed during January, 1963, before a reconstruction scheme was carried out. The fountain had been erected in 1868 in memory of William Gibson, merchant, Maulesbank, who was instrumental in bringing a water supply to the community. It stood on the site of an old public well.

In February, 1963. Mr Alfred Sim, London, made a gift of Charles Cundall's painting of Arbroath harbour to the town. It was accepted by Provost D.A. Gardner. Our picture shows the painting being admired in the Town House by, from left - Bailie R.R. Spink, Bailie J.M. McBain, Mr W.D. Smith, Town Clerk; Bailie F.W.A. Thornton and Provost Gardner.

In February, 1963, shopkeepers in Keptie Street, West Port, Brothock Bridge and Commerce Street launched the West End Traders' Association and one of their first actions was to petition Arbroath Town Council to ensure the best possible bus service for the municipal housing scheme in the west end of the town, at Timmergreens. Pictured at the inaugural meeting are, from left, back - Mr D. Bruce, Mr William B. Booth, A.K. Adamson's; Mr George A. Jervie, chairman, Robertson's Chemist; and Mr Cherry Hunter, Hunter Butcher: front - Mr Fred Leslie, Campbell Electrician; Miss Margaret Robbie, Robbie's newsagency; and Mr Andrew Brown, A. W. Brown's grocery.

Mrs Jane Lowe, the oldest member of the Culloden Ladies' Club, cuts the cake at the club's birthday party in March, 1963. At the table are, from left - Mrs P.M. Hayes, president; Mrs Ala Rodgers, Mrs Goodwillie, Mrs Mollison, -------- and Mrs Buick.

At the beginning of April, 1963, Arbroath's Territorial Army WRAC platoon, part of the famous 51st Highland Division, held its first passing out parade in the Drill Hall, Marketgate, now the Community Centre. The inspecting officer was Brigadier J.A. Oliver, West Newton, Arbroath, who also presented certificates to the 13 members of the platoon who were on parade. He was accompanied by Lieutenant-Colonel Lady Martha Bruce, commanding officer of the 51st Highland Division WRAC (TA). Our picture shows, from left, back row - Winnie Saddler, Margaret McArdle, Annie Littlejohn, Margaret Reid, June Lime and Moira Gillespie: middle row - Sheila Coutts, Janet Moir, Lily Mason, Elma Bews, Moira Scott, Edna Beattie and Laura Taylor: front row - Sergeant Heeney, Lady Bruce, Brigadier Oliver, Lieutenant Hart and Sergeant Major McCallum.

Supermarket chain, Lipton's, decided to include Arbroath in its portfolio of modern grocery shops and in April, 1963, the new store opened at 226 High Street. The opening attracted a huge crowd as the 'guest of honour' was Rosie, Brooke Bond's famous chimpanzee. Although not hugely removed from what we see in today's interpretation of customer self-service, Lipton's store retained more of a personal touch which was characteristic of the first generation of the new style-shopping. In our picture, the manager of the facility, Mr J. MacDonald, looks on as a member of staff packs frozen food into a freezer cabinet.

This bustling High Street scene, looking from Kirk Square in the direction of Guthrie Port, was photographed on a sunny day at the beginning of May, 1963, and will give the latest generation of Arbroathians an idea of what the town's main shopping street was like before it was pedestrianised. At the left foreground, a group of workmen from the Royal Burgh of Arbroath Roads Department are laying kerbing, making use of a combined digger and conveyor tractor unit. The police officer on the opposite corner is thought to be Walter Hutcheon, who later became Superintendent in charge of Arbroath Police. The shop the workmen are congregated in front of is Hepworth's, and the businesses stretching along the left side of the street are - the former Lipton's shop, the business having already moved up the street; Boots the chemist; Millar's of Broughty Ferry, ladies' outfitter; Wm Low's supermarket; Swankie's fish, fruit and flowers shop, at 170 High Street; Pert, house furnishers, and Pert's Babyland, 176 High Street; Porteous, bakers; the Bon Accord Cafe, run by Ian Grant, and, on the corner of Applegate, Menzies, newsagent and bookseller. Across Applegate were - A. Mair, fruiterer; Hunter, cobblers; D.A. Sanderson, baker, 206 High Street; R.S. Cargill, confectioner, ice cream manufacturer and cafe, 212 High Street; The Hosiery; the new Lipton shop; Lefevre, tobacconist, 236 High Street; Bennett, chemist; and Don Robertson, licensed retailer, taking us to the Lordburn junction. On the other side of High Street, starting from the Kirk Square corner, were - Geddes, ladies' outfitter; Stewart, butcher; Grant, house furnisher; J.K. Moir, The Shakespeare Bar; Phillip's Wool Shop; A. Sangster, jeweller, at 189 High Street; Munro, butcher; Scott, family grocer, owned and run by Alex Napier; Salmond's bakery; and, on the corner of High Street and Allan Street, Milne's butcher shop.

An extensive improvement scheme for Brothock Bridge was begun at the end of January, 1963, when work to replace the roof of the bridge got underway. However, the project was not without problems, as the 120-year-old stone arch declined to give way graciously and proved almost impervious to modern demolition machinery. Our picture shows the stage the construction had reached by early summer with steel reinforced concrete beams laid on concrete buttresses to replace the arched stone bridge. The work was undertaken by Ian C. Hunter Ltd, Contractor.

Members of Arbroath Instrumental Band pictured following a practise session at the band hall in Helen Street in 1963. They are, from left, back --------, Tom Cargill, Yvonne Smith, Anne Gerrard, Douglas Wright, Ray Will, William Boyle, Nancy Goodwillie and George Willisonson: middle row - Tom Peebles, Gordon Goodwillie, Vic Lewis, Tim Berry, Alex Petrie, Colin Smith, Raymond Stuart, Ian Cargill and Ferg Lundie: front row - Willie Jarret, Fred Crowe, Ed Harrison jnr, Jack Boyle, bandmaster; Ernie Gerrard, Ed Harrison and Fred Moseley.

To mark the centenary of the Red Cross Society, a service of dedication was held in Arbroath's Old Parish Church on Sunday, May 5, 1963. Arbroath Voluntary Aid Detachment (VAD), under Miss Jean Cuthill, and Carnoustie VAD, led by Mrs Nita McDougall, paraded to the church where the service was conducted by the Rev. T. Gemmell Campbell. Among those in attendance were, from left - Miss Cuthill, commandant Arbroath VAD; Miss Margaret Thomson, cadet officer, Arbroath; Mrs Mary Beedie, assistant commandant, Arbroath; Miss Violet Morrison, nursing superintendent, Arbroath; Miss Margaret Ross, assistant commandant, Carnoustie VAD; Miss Margaret Peters, assistant cadet officer, Arbroath; and Mrs McDougall, commandant Carnoustie VAD.

This aerial picture from 1963 illustrates just how much has gone from the centre of Arbroath in the intervening years. At the bottom of the picture is Hill Street, with Commerce Street at bottom left and Boulzie Hill at right. High Street runs up the middle past Arbroath Abbey and on to Guthrie Port and St Andrew's Church. The large building in the centre foreground was formerly the Picture House cinema, now Gala Bingo with the Old Parish Church in Kirk Square just beyond. The complex of industrial buildings shows Keith Blackman Ltd., fan engineers, middle left, between High Street and Gravesend, with Douglas Fraser & Sons, engineers, at top left. The new high-rise blocks in Wardmill Road Barngreen, Smithy Croft and Guthrie Hill are prominent at centre top, although some vestiges of the Wyndies, which they replaced, remain.

Page 55

In October, 1963, Sir James A.L. Duncan, MP for South Angus, was presented with the Freedom of Arbroath at a ceremony in the Webster Memorial Hall in appreciation of the services he had rendered to the community as Member of Parliament. Sir James received a framed Burgess Ticket from Provost D.A. Gardner. Our picture shows Sir James and Lady Duncan with Provost Gardner in the front row setting off from the Town House to the Webster Hall, the parade being led by Town Officer Bill Fairweather and Dundee City Officer, F.R. Jenkins. In the second row are Mr Tom Connell, sole survivor of the 28 local Boer War veterans made Freemen on their return from that conflict, and the Hon. J.S. Maclay, former MP for the old Montrose Burghs constituency, made a Freeman in 1950. The third row comprises Captain K.R. Hickson, commanding officer of HMS Condor, upon which the Freedom of the town was conferred in 1961, and Sheriff Principal G.C. Emslie. They are followed by Town Councillors, Burgh officials and guests.

Office bearers of Arbroath Burns Club and guests at the 1964 Burns Supper in Hotel Seaforth. In the picture are, from left, back - Neil Macmillan, William Rae, D. L. Gardiner, A. Bisset, David Goodwillie, honorary treasurer; David McKechnie, William Somerville, William Macdonald and Jack Lamb: front - Councillor David Chapel, Provost D.A. Gardner, Eric B. Mackintosh, Thomas Leslie, Broughty Ferry, who proposed the Immortal Memory; Thomas H. Mann, president; ex-Provost John F. Webster, James B. Crockatt and G. Donaldson.

Members of the ladies' chorus of Arbroath Amateur Operatic Society's production of 'Brigadoon' staged in the Webster Hall in February, 1964. They are, from left, back - A. McEwing, F. Smith, Jess Hogg, Joan Mitchell, Grace Allen, Evelyn Robertson, Evelyn Malcolm, Marian Farquhar, Irene Scott and Joan Vale: front - Valerie Scott, Heather Harbour, M. Peter, Elaine Seroczynska and Nancy Todd.

The first steps in the establishment of a permanent public collection of fine embroidery in Arbroath was taken at the Public Library on Saturday, March 21, 1964, when an oak case, specially constructed to house the initial collection was handed over by Arbroath Embroidery Club to the Library Committee. Pictured at the ceremony in the Arbroath Room are, from left - Mr Norman Crawford, librarian; Mrs U.R. Shaw, Mrs J. Matthew, Mrs A.K. Adamson, Mr W.L. Reid and Mrs E. Patterson.

Senior dancers of the Appolinari School of Dance with their tutors and guest artistes prior to the annual show in the Webster Hall in 1964. Pictured are, from left, back - Rosa Appolinari, Elizabeth Kinnear, Colin Smith, Roland Cruickshanks and Conway Stuart: front - Anne Verth, Marianne Cargill, Edwina Gillespie, Yvonne Smith and Jennifer Bogulak.

Page 60

Arbroath Amateur Boxing Club was still a fledgling organisation when this picture was taken in April, 1964, but had already attracted a large membership of enthusiastic youngsters who were coached by brothers, Dave and Doug Ford and Jack Hall. Our picture was taken at a training session in the premises of the former National Bank at Brothock Bank House which was situated across the road from the Arbroath Herald building. Pictured are, from left, back - Jim Spink, Jack Hall, Eddie Keillor, --- Simpson, Robbie Ronald, Dave Ford, --------, Russell Ruxton, Drummond Hall, Peter Cunningham, Alan McFarlane, Dave Thomson, Ian Cooper, Andy Cargill, Joe McLeod and Doug Ford: front - Alan Miller, --------, Freddie Oldfield and Robin Hall.

The tracks of the old harbour branch railway between Catherine Street and Shore in the course of being removed in September, 1964. Our picture shows workmen lifting the section from the Millgate crossing, with the operation to take out the lines from Catherine Street having been completed. The work was done manually, with the lines cut into small sections. The area is still affectionately referred to as 'The Linies' and is now a free car park. The Stag Bar is visible to the left of the picture, where a passer-by pauses to scrutinise the work being undertaken. To the near right are the photographic premises of the late Ian Wight now occupied by games and toys retailer, GMV. Across Millgate, beside the chatting ladies, is a corner of the Victoria Cafe with its snooker room upstairs, now the Saffron Indian restaurant. In the distance, to the right, is the former factory of Francis Webster & Sons, Ltd., sailmakers, on ground now occupied by the Weavers Close housing development.

Arbroath High School girls' tennis team during 1964 comprised, from left, back - Monica Page, Elizabeth Connelly and Christine Robertson: front - Islay McDougall, Alma Ruark and Patricia Boyack.

Page 63

In May, 1964, a special party was held at Cliff House Residential Home to mark the 98th birthday of Miss Margaret Scott, who is seen cutting her birthday cake. On her left is matron, Mrs Lena Scott, with her assistant, Miss Marina Rodgers. Sharing the celebration were, at right, Mrs Helen Watson, who was 82, and Miss Hannah Smith, who was 90.

Eminent people from all parts of Scotland assembled in the Civil Hall of the Gatehouse Range at Arbroath Abbey on June 26, 1964, to mark the 650th anniversary of the Battle of Bannockburn in appropriate style and setting. The distinguished company included, from left, back - Mr George B. Lowe, managing director, Arbroath Herald; Mr J. Sturrock, Arbroath Abbey custodian; ex-Provost D.A. Gardner, Arbroath; Mr Comyn Webster, editor, The Scottish Field; Mr Noel Stevenson, controller, Scottish Television; Mr John Chisholm, Arbroath publicity officer; Bailie F.W.A. Thornton, co-producer, Arbroath Abbey Pageant; Mr David Kinnaird, British Broadcasting Corporation and a member of Arbroath Summer Show company; Mr Kenneth Peters, managing editor, Aberdeen Journals; Mr Thomas E. Buncle, managing director, Arbroath Guide; Mr Wilfred Taylor, columnist, The Scotsman; the Rev T. Gemmell Campbell, Arbroath Old Parish Church and a member of the executive of the Pageant Society; Mr P.M. Hayes, editor, Arbroath Guide; Councillor Joe Riley, Pageant executive; Mr R.A. Daw, editor, Scots Magazine; and Mr Keith Fraser, chairman of Arbroath Publicity Council: front - Mr W.A. Nicholson, manager and secretary, Scottish Tourist Board; Mr George S. Shepherd, editor, Arbroath Herald and co-producer of the Pageant; Mr Andy Stewart, Mr A. Linton Robertson, chairman of the Pageant Society; Provost Robert R. Spink, Sir John Ure Primrose and Mr Eric B. Mackintosh, secretary of the Pageant Society. Centrepiece of the table decoration was the bronze head of Robert Bruce by Mr C. d'O Pilkington Jackson, which shortly before had been gifted to Arbroath Public Library.

Cast members of the 1964 production of Arbroath Abbey Pageant pictured within Arbroath Abbey during a rehearsal in June of that year. They are, from left, back row - Joe Riley, Ally Rintoull, Jimmy Milne, Fergus Ellen, Neil McLeod, Gordon Moir, Bill McGugan, Blair Morison and Allan Wallace: middle row - Bill ------, D.Y. Walker, John Mentiply, --------, William McDougall, Philip Melville, Neil Melville, Douglas Cant, Stewart Newton, Bill Shaw, Brian Hosie, --------, Ken ------, --------, Jack Laing, Harry Whitton, Bruce Matthews, --------, --- Gourlay, --------, Arthur Kerr, Joe Duncan, Jeff Dugdale, Alex Keith, Alistair Martin and Ken McDonald: front row - Sandy Keith, Morris Pert, Tony Wishart, Jim McGugan and Donald (or Sandy) Fraser.

Members of Arbroath Sporting Club (ASC) just a year or two after the club was formed. In those days it played in the Angus Juvenile League. Some of those pictured took part in the Scottish Juvenile Cup final against Lochee Renton at Gayfield Park and Thomson Park during season 1964/65. The Dundee side won both legs 5-3 with Jimmy Jack, who signed for Arbroath the following year, netting a hat-trick for Lochee at Gayfield. Pictured are, from left, back - Frank McEwan, Gordon Stewart, Steve Myles, Jim Clark, Tompie Stephens and Gordon Lorimer: front - Ray Thomson, Jimmy Fairweather, Norman Miller, Dave Lyall and Dave Smith.

Arbroath High School footballers from 1964. They are, from left, back - Dave Vannet, Kenny Head, Alan Stott, Alan Campbell, Stewart Mackay and John Campbell: front - John Breckenridge, Alex Bates, William Ross, William Low and David Stewart.

Members of Inverkeilor WRI Concert Party in 1964. They are, from left, standing - Mrs Gertie Milne, Mrs Jean McIntosh, Ruby Hay, Mrs Ann Hutcheon, Mrs Agnes Stewart, Mrs Margaret Reid and Mrs Isa Breckenridge: seated - Mrs ---- Arthur, Mrs Ann Wight, Mrs Moira Harrow, Mrs Ruby Alexander, Mrs Margaret Kydd, Mrs Jean Coull and Mrs Helen McIntosh.

The 7th Arbroath Boys' Brigade in 1964 won the inaugural 'Sportagama' cup, a major event on the BB calendar, for a 10-minute musical act of entertainment. The event was held at Arbroath Academy, and among those responsible for the boys' victory that year were, from left - Lieutenant Betty Greenhowe, Liz Kinnear, pianist; Lieutenant Earl Matthew, Lieutenant Diana Christie and Lieutenant Beatrice Gerrard. The cup was won in competition against 12 companies of the Angus Battalion. The 7th Arbroath presented a cancan routine, with the boys taking the part of the dancing girls.

Gentlemen of the 'Fourth Estate' in Arbroath enjoy themselves at a press party in about 1965. They are, from left - J. Quentin Clark, Dundee Courier; Clark Massey, Dundee Courier; Nor Riddle, Arbroath Herald; Innes Irvine, Arbroath Guide; Doug Pratt, Arbroath Guide; and George S. Shepherd, Arbroath Herald editor.

This picture of members of Arbroath Round Table, with wives and guests, was taken in about 1965, in, we think, the Monkbarns Hotel. Present are, from left, back - Gill Dickie, David Cargill, Innes Irvine, Derry Sangster, George Ramsay, Rae Forrester, --- Sutherland, Sandy Milne, Bill Rae and Peter Black: middle - Ella Hunter, Jean Dickie, Ella Cargill, Lily Wight and Pat Milne: front - Lorna Parker, Ann Black, Margaret Rae, Eunice Sutherland, Mae Irvine, Hilda Forrester and Isabel Ramsay.

Members of 2422 (Arbroath) Squadron, Air Training Corps, pictured in the Sea Cadet Hall, Arrott Street, in 1965. They are, from left, back row - John Rae, George Edgar, Ian Waldie, Allan Metcalfe, Allan Marnie, Fraser Balharrie, Craig Burnett, Alan Ramsay, George Findlay and Jim Bell: middle row - Keith Robertson, Brian Laybourne, Robert Beattie, Ian Eddie, Ewan Hayes, Dennis Meecham, Donald Miller, Allan Duncan and Steve Miller: front row - Malcolm Finlayson, Derek Lowson, Pilot Officer John Vernon, Pilot Officer Gordon Smart, Flying Officer Alan Southcott, Warrant Officer Jim Penman, Jim Nangle and George Penman.

In March, 1965, Arbroath Ladies' Choir engaged as their guest the Australian opera star, John Cameron, baritone, who had twice previously sung with Arbroath Male Voice Choir. Pictured at their concert are, from left, front row - Mrs May Lawson, Mrs Jenny Petrie, president; Miss Annie Doig Winter, accompanist; Mr John Cameron, Miss Ruth Morrison, choir accompanist; Mr Andrew Morrison, conductor; Mrs Muriel Steven, secretary; and Mrs Cath Hebenton, librarian; second row - Mrs Alicia Greig, Mrs Isobel Robertson, Miss Frances Rooney, Mrs Rita Morrison, Mrs Catherine Lumgair, Miss M. Taylor, Mrs Cissie Fleming, Mrs Isobel Knowles, Miss Irene Hunter, Miss Margaret Hunter, Mrs May Anderson and Mrs Annie Cochrane; back row - Mrs Ada McNaughton, Mrs Helen King, Mrs Vera McFarlane, Mrs Margaret Lumgair, Mrs Helen Young, Mrs Margo Barlow, Mrs Florence Rae, Mrs Helen Ross, Mrs J. Millar, Miss Peggy Mitchell, Miss Eleanor Munro, Miss C. Petrie and Miss S. Sharp.

Page 74

At a special service in Arbroath's Old Parish Church on Sunday, April 11, 1965, part of the optical apparatus which had been in operation at the Bell Rock Lighthouse between 1901 and 1963 was presented to the church for safe keeping. The lens frame bore the marks of German bullets following an attack on the light by aircraft during the Second World War. Pictured at the handover ceremony are, from left - the Rev. T. Gemmell Campbell, Mr D. Alan Stevenson, a great grandson of Robert Stevenson who built the lighthouse; Mrs Stevenson, Mr W. Alistair Robertson, general manager and secretary of the Northern Lighthouses Board; Provost R.R. Spink and Mr James Rae, a member of the church, who made the case to house the apparatus.

Members of Arbroath Abbey Theatre Club rehearse for their production of Sutton Vane's 'Outward Bound' which was staged in the Arbroath's 'little theatre' in April, 1965. They are, from left, standing - Shona McGreavey, prompter; T. Burns Mitchell, producer; Arthur Kerr, Alistair Cameron, Ken Cargill, Nancy Henderson and Jack Laing: seated - Alison Harvey, Marlene Kear and Bill Shaw.

In this view of the new Elms housing development, taken in April, 1965, three generations of local housing styles are to be seen. In the background is the mansion house, The Elms, in the middle distance the remaining housing in the post-war prefab scheme being cleared away and, at left foreground, a corner of an old people's housing block in Elmfield Crescent.

This group shows *Arbroath Herald* staff in May, 1965, when they honoured foreman printer, Willie Robertson (centre left), on the occasion of his retiral after 33 years' service to the company. He is seen being presented with a gold watch by Mr George B. Lowe, managing director, and he also received an ornamental glass-domed clock from his colleagues. Looking on in the company's printing department are, from left - Dave McKenzie, Stewart Donaldson, --------, Jean Rennie, Dave Fairweather, Marjory Ross, Cath McDonald, Carol Gibbon, Colin Archer, Jim Dempster, Ron Cargill, Norman Melville, Bob Smith, Bobby Ross, Jim Holmes, Ian Berrie, Donald Forbes, Jimmy Milne and Dave Melville.

Pupils of class 2A at Arbroath Academy in 1965. They are, from left, back row - Alec Spink, Dave Cargill, Ken Graham, Bill Swankie, Alec McDonald, Bill Allison, Hugh Payne and Graham Moir: second row - Gus Menmuir, Alan Nelson, Jim Smith, Stephen Deacon, Dave Swankie, Bob Nicol, Brian Cooper, Bill Masson and Lindsay Milne: third row - Marion Hind, Lynda Black, Brenda Beattie, Cherille Reid, Jenny Welsh, Dorothy Taylor, Cheryl Rayfield, Hazel Allan, Francis Officer, Aileen Swankie and Elizabeth Roessler: front row - Moyra Smith, Pat Dyer, Irene Beattie, Pat Forsythe, Jackie Cargill, Sheila Willox, Beryl Robertson, Valerie Massie and Joyce McIntosh.

Left - Newsreel cameras were in place and a large crowd, of which our picture shows only a small part, had gathered outside the Town House on Wednesday, July 21, 1965, for a ceremonial march-past by officers and men of HMS Condor, at that time an operational naval air station, to mark the 25th anniversary of the base being commissioned. Captain R.H. Webber and Provost R.R. Spink took the salute. Our picture, taken from the saluting base in front of the Town House and looking towards Commerce Street, highlights the small group of shops there. At the corner was the premises of John Lamb, butcher, which was later acquired by East Angus Co-operative Society and then Wilson Family Butchers. It is now the offices of Connolly and Yeoman, solicitors. Next door, the former Cafe Gibson changed hands numerous times having become a licensed premises in the process. It, too is now in use as office accommodation. The Scottish Gas showroom and office, later British Gas, survived until the late 1980s and now houses Independent Financial Services Ltd. The shoe shop of Charles Reid, at 86 High Street, operated until the early 1970s when Mr Reid retired and the premises was acquired by Yule newsagents about 1975. Early in 2004 the business was purchased by Mr Reehan Ul-haq on the retiral of Sandy Yule. Above - HMS Condor personnel march down Arbroath High Street, 'bayonets fixed, drums beating and Colours flying', as a privilege granted to the Royal Naval Air Station when they received the Freedom of the Burgh four years previously. This picture shows A.A.3 Hendry with the framed Burgess Ticket escorted by A.A.3 Lugg and A.A.3 Northcote as they passed the Town House for the salute which was taken by Captain A.H. Webster and Provost Robert R. Spink.

Officials and members of Lochlands Bowling Club pose for the first formal picture in front of their new pavilion in July, 1965. They are, from left, back row - William Petrie, James Birse, Jack Coutts, James Stewart, William Farquhar, James Hudgston, --------, George Patterson, Peter Jamieson, Alf Carr, William Christie, George Nicol and Alfred Hardie: second row - David Spink, James Simpson, -------- and David Anderson: third row - Andrew Cargill, Alan Robertson, William Burnett, James Oram, James Nicol, David Hudgston, George White, David Rae, Archibald McIntosh, William Smith, Jack Christie, James Smith, --------, Fred Taylor and James Stephen: front row - David Carrie, Ron Rennie, George Jamieson, Martin Mostyn, Walter Laverie, George Gardner, William McKie, George B. Anderson, Ron Smith, David Kydd and Alexander Gray.

Page 82

At the end of August, 1965, there were 1,400 entries for Arbroath and District Horticultural Society and Floral Art Group's annual show held in the Drill Hall, Marketgate. The Blue Riband was won by Dundee schoolteacher, Mr A.A. Simpson with a magnificent collection of vegetables. Our group taken at the opening of the event by Lady Ogilvy shows, from left - Mrs Shirley Mathieson, Lady Ogilvy, Brigadier James A. Oliver, Mrs Oliver and Provost R.R. Spink.

Past presidents of Arbroath Fisherman's Association sat for this formal group in 1965. A few fishboxes were to hand to provide seats for those in the front row! Pictured are, from left, back - James Cargill (Cannie's Jeemie's Jim), 1957 to '59; Adam Cargill (Big Ad), 1945 to '46; Thomas Beattie, 1963 to '65; Peter Cargill (Nellie Eaton's Peter), 1954 to '56; John Swankie (John Polar), 1951 to '53; John Smith (Shirkie's John), 1960 to '62; and William Swankie (Polar's Bill), 1937 to '39: front - Daniel Cargill (Cannie's Danny), 1940 to '41; Peter Shepherd (Peter the Beel), 1942 to '44; David Beattie (Malopus), 1933 to '36; William Bruce (Willie Brisie), 1925 to '26; Joseph Cargill (Adam's Joe), 1927 to '28; and Robert Smith (Shirkie's Bob), 1929 to '32.

Officials and guests of Arbroath Burns Club at the annual Burns Supper in Hotel Seaforth on Friday, January 28, 1966. They are, from left, back - Mr David McKechnie, Mr A.K. Bissett, Mr Colin Archer, Mr John Bryce, the Rev. Archibald Russell, Mr John McGregor, Mr E. McFerran, Piper David McKenzie, the Rev. T. Gemmell Campbell, Mr George S. Shepherd, Mr William Rae and Mr D. Somerville: front - Mr R.C. Matthew, Mr J.B. Crockatt, Provost Robert R. Spink, Mr Tom Mann, president; Mr Edwin O. Hector, who proposed The Immortal Memory; Mr Neil McMillan, Mr Ralph Kraut, president of Giddings & Lewis, Fond du Lac, Wisconsin, USA; and Mr David S. Moyes, Carnoustie.

Members of Arbroath Male Voice Choir and their guests, Jean Allister, contralto, and Edgar Fleet, her tenor husband, following their annual concert in the Webster Hall in February, 1966. Pictured are, from left, back row - Alec Keith, James Paterson, John Thomson, Joe Riley, Bill Wright, Jack W. Fleming, Bill Kydd, Ed Cant, Jim Begg, Frank Wyllie, D. Sinclair, Harry J. Davidson, Harry Farmer, David Ferguson, James Webster, Joe Duncan and J. Jeffrey: second row - Tom Mitchell, David Mitchell, Alec Wood, Ally Lindsay, Allan Caird, Alec Watt, Ian Whyte, Charles Smith, Bob Kydd, Alec Millar, William McDougall, John Petrie and Ralph Duncan: front row - George Petrie, Alec Ramsay, Bob Ferguson, Terry Myles, William Cant, Miss Annie Doig Winter, Edgar Fleet, Jean Allister, Andrew Morrison, conductor; Mrs Winnie Sangster and Graham Hamilton.

Footballers of the 5th Arbroath (Abbey Church) Company of the Boys' Brigade, who won the Arbroath Boys' Brigade League Cup and the Angus Junior Five-a-Side Trophy in 1966 pictured with their silverware. The youngsters are, from left, back - Ronald Bell, Ian Bell, Patrick Mann, David Cromar, Alan Giles, Mike Giles, Brian Pankhurst and Tommy Walker: front - Neil Christie, Colin Cromar, Ian Monroe, Ian Thoms, Ian Stott, Ally Bennett and Graham Moir.

In March, 1966, the impressive new Arbroath and District Indoor Bowling Stadium in Cairnie Road was opened by Arbroath's own radio, stage and television personality, Andy Stewart. The event attracted guests from all over Angus, Dundee, Perth, Aberdeen and Glasgow. The two-storey building, which cost £60,000, contained eight rinks, a well-equipped restaurant to seat 100 people and a bar. In our picture, Mrs Sheila Stewart is seen throwing the first jack watched by, from left - Mr James G. Cronshaw, chairman of the board of directors of the enterprise; Andy Stewart and Mr John Greig, manager.

In May, 1966, the Royal Artillery celebrated its 250th anniversary with a series of events throughout the country. In Arbroath, the local unit, Q Battery, 400 Field Regiment, RA(T), organised a cocktail party, a mounted parade through the town, a drumhead service and, pictured here, a reunion lunch in the Montrose Road headquarters. Included in the picture are, from left, top table - Joe Wood, snr, Jock Innes, George Rennie, --------, Niall Pattullo, Len Gregory, Jim Bowron, --------, Colonel C.N. Thomson, Major J.G. Mathieson, TD, battery commander; Hugh Fraser, Lieutenant-Colonel G.R.L. Barron, MC, commanding officer; Andy Watt, Fred Cossans, Dave Blues, Lyndon Bolton, Sandy Christie and Bill McPhee: back row - Bob Aitken, Jim Coutts, Larry Falconer and Dave Rennie: third row - George Ritchie, Bill White, Dennis Smith, --------, -- Holden, Lindsay Taylor, Chae Glen, Jock Adam, Charlie Ogilvie, Bill Tindal, Alec Smith and Jim Stott: second row - Bill Begg, Jock Russell, Jack Morrison, Bob Nicoll, Bill Eaton, Doug Petrie, Joe Wood, Alan Brand, Colin Beattie, Jim Taylor, Duncan Tasker, Bill Cadger, Dave Stott and --------: front row - Bob Bridges, --------, Norman Livie, Fred Robb, Jock Graham, Fred Mitchell, John Cargill, Jim Manzie, --------, Roy Fitchet, Derry Anderson, George Watson, Derek Miller and Brian Williams.

Arbroath's town clerk, Mr W.D. Smith, who had served the burgh for 21 years, departed in May, 1966, to take up the post of depute county clerk for Midlothian. At a ceremony in the town house he was presented with a J. McIntosh Patrick painting of Auchmithie by Provost R.R. Spink on behalf of the town council and the people of Arbroath. Earlier, in his own department, he had received farewell gifts of Edinburgh crystal glasses and a jug from the youngest member of staff, Kathleen Macdonald. In our picture are, from left - Bailie Frank Thornton, Provost Spink, Mr Smith, Councillor Adam Cargill and Mr George Rodger, burgh engineer.

Boys of forms V and VI at Arbroath High School in 1966. They are, from left, back row - Jim Smith, Eddie Smith, David Goodwillie, Chae Dawson, Alex Gibson and Robert Southwell: second row - Geoff Duncan, Morris Pert, Pete Smith, Norman Menmuir, Bill Findlay, Allan Tunstall, Roy Walker, Les Wood, David Crockett and Ian Chisholm: third row - Dave Clark, Russell Robertson, Alex Small, Duncan Finlayson, Eddie Marnie, Derek Lowson, Andy Clark, Dave Cromar, Ian Cowie, Derek Cluckie, Willie Fairlie, James Hall and Ian Gracie: front row - Colin Armstrong, Tony Laing, Jeff Dugdale, John Campbell, David Thornton, Jim Graham, Rector Hay, Sandy Keith, Philip Teale, David Bridges, Ian Young, Bob Smith and Colin Harper.

How little acorns can grow into giant oaks! Our picture shows the Meadow Milk Bar at the site of the Meadowbank Inn. Opened in 1966, when our picture was taken, the facility was the brainchild of local farmer and footballer, Ian Stirling. As well as refreshing milk-based drinks, a variety of fresh farm produce was also on offer. The milk bar eventually gave way to the range of buildings we see on the site today.

Members of class 4G at Arbroath Academy in 1966 were, from left, back row - Elizabeth Smith, Petula Sim, Dorothy Anderson, Wilena Wood, Aileen Proctor, Sheila Cunningham, Christine Bolton, Elizabeth Gray and Linda Forest: second row - Elizabeth Wilson, Irene Milne, Edna Goodwin, Arlene Geddes, Jessie Kidd, Marie Knowles, Iris Teviotdale, Irene Middleton and Julie Donald: third row - Maureen Pyper, Hazel Anderson, Jackie Irons, Eva Cooper, Barbara Grant, Linda Martin, Joyce Lorimer, Aileen Pearson and Carol Swankie: front row - Isobel Gordon, Rona Leadingham, Catherine Lindsay, Francis Eddy, Irene Thom, Kay Hall, Margaret Swankie, Denise Cowe and Maureen Fincham.

For many years, Copland's Garage, which stood at the junction of Cairnie Street and Lochlands Drive, was one of the town's principal taxi firms. This photograph, taken in 1966, shows a line-up of taxis, all the standard 'London' FX4 model. Also in the picture is proprietor, Mr Bert Copland, with a Morris Oxford which was his pride and joy. The garage was founded in 1943 by Mr Copland who originally ran it on a part-time basis from a wooden shed on the site, while also working for Messrs Shanks, where he drove for the firm and maintained the owner's Bentley and Aston Martin cars. The shed was bought from T. Hood, market gardener. The building in the picture, built around 1950, was demolished about 1995. The taxis were bought second-hand, and, judging by the registrations, they came from sources as diverse as London, Aberdeen and Glasgow. The fleet also included a 1934 Rolls Royce, used principally for weddings, but not above being utilised for taxi duties when the firm was busy. The ground to the far right, across Lochlands Drive, was the site of Blindloch Dairy, and is now occupied by Lochlands Gardens.

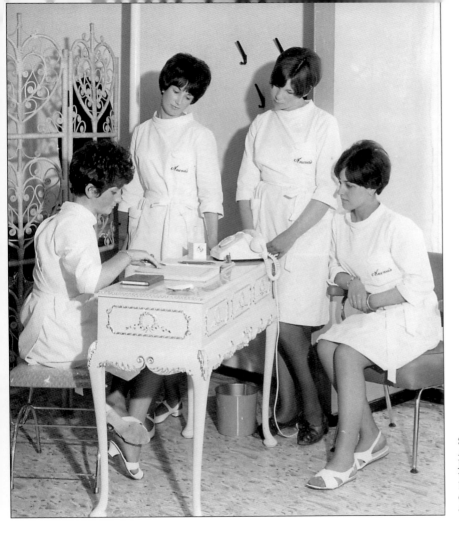

Staff at the Arbroath hairstyling establishment of Anona's, 18 Keptie Street, when the business opened in July, 1966. At left is the prorietrix, Miss Anona Smith, with her apprentices, from left - Marie-Anne Edwards, Lesley Henderson and Maria Turner. The premises originally housed a grocer's shop, then became a florists and before a major renovation was a car spares outlet.

In September, 1966, work began on the demolition of buildings at the corner of High Street and Abbey Path which included the Oriental Bar. In June 22, 1897, at the time of the Diamond Jubilee of Queen Victoria, the Oriental was owned by Mr D.A. Gouck, who was in charge until 1900, when the bar was taken over by Ralph Gouck, perhaps his son. He in turn, was licensee until 1907, when Mr G.K. Black acquired the public house and he ran it for almost 20 years, until 1925, when it was taken over by Mr Alex McIntosh. However, his tenure was short, as a new owner, Mr William Baillie, is noted only one year later. He ran the business until 1938, when it was taken over by H. Coburn, who had over ten years in charge, until William McKenzie took over in 1950/51. Three years later, James Muirhead became the licensee and he was followed by Tom Swankie, a weel kent Fit o' the Toon personality, who was a member of the lifeboat crew. The final owner was Mr William Coutts, who took over in October, 1964. For a short time, he and his wife ran both the Oriental Bar and the National Bar, just a short distance away on the other side of High Street, which they bought when the Oriental was sold to a development company in June, 1966.

Youngsters of St Thomas RC Primary School football team in 1966. They are, from left, standing - Joe Brown, Alan Bekier, James Logue, Tony Smith, Chris Plawecki and Martin Roy: seated - Peter Bowie, Gavin Mylles, Stephen Beattie, Frank Orsi and Steven Mylles: front - George Webster and Brian Lindsay.

Giddings & Lewis-Fraser Ltd, once Arbroath's biggest employer, was presented with the Queen's Award to Industry in September, 1966, in recognition of their achievements in the export field. The award was handed over at a ceremony in the firm's new £50,000 extension in Orchard Street by Lord Ogilvy, who was deputising for his father, the Earl of Airlie, Lord Lieutenant of Angus. Our picture will bring back memories for the workforce of the time. It shows activity in the assembly bay, where machinery is packaged prior to transport. In the background are stacks of packing cases ready to go and the men are working crating textile machinery for shipment to Pakistan.

The ladies of the dancing troupe who took part in Arbroath Amateur Operatic Society's presentation of 'The Merry Widow' in the Webster Theatre in February, 1967. They are, from left - Kay Smith, Elaine Masson, who was also choreographer; Marianne Edwards, Sheena Guthrie, Elaine Seroczynska, Edna Nicoll, Edwina Gillespie and Margaret McLaren.

Taken in March, 1967, this picture illustrates how the quiet urban haven of the red sandstone houses in the area between Ladyloan and Millgate was shattered in the name of progress for the construction of the so called 'internal bypass'. At the extreme left, the two-storey house was at the top of Glover Street, and it and the line of single-storey dwellings with dormer windows made up the top portion of the street, to its junction with Hannah Street. The three-storey building to the right of centre is part of Nicollie's Mill at the corner of East Mary Street and Chalmers Street, the site now occupied by the JobCentre. The three tall chimneys on the skyline are, from left, those of Burnside Mill, between Gravesend and Brothock Bridge; the Arbroath Herald and Arbroath Public Baths, Marketgate. All have long been demolished.

A popular hostelry at the Fit o' the Toon was the Bell Rock Tavern, at the corner of West Grimsby and John Street West. It was thought to have been converted some time in the late 18th or early 19th century from a single storey cottage built with sea bools. It became a tavern in those flourishing days when Arbroath harbour was so crowded with fishing and trading craft that you could almost walk across it on a floor of boats. Some of its first customers might have been the masons who prepared the stones which were shipped out to the Bell Rock when the lighthouse was being constructed in the early years of the 19th century. During the years of the Second World War, not only local fishermen, but also servicemen billeted in the town patronised the Bell Rock Tavern and all were insulted as friends by the vociferous Amazonian parrot kept in the bar by the proprietors, Bill and Margaret Taylor. The thing that caught everyone's eye was the emblem above the main door which showed a coloured rendition of the Inchcape Rock and the bell the Abbot of Aberbrothock had put there to warn mariners of the danger. Meekison the painter was given the task of seeing it was kept in good order. The building and all its neighbours were demolished to make way for the new dual carriageway through the centre of the town.

In 1967, the North of Scotland Hydro Electric Board's North District depot was the former power generating facility in South Grimsby which was demolished some months later to make way for the dual carriageway. It had previously been run by Grampian Electric Light and Power which generated DC current on steam driven generators. The tall condensation towers, used to turn the steam back into water, were local landmarks. Electricity was generated there right up to the 1950s, until AC power from the National Grid had been delivered to every house. However, the changeover was gradual, one street, and sometimes even one house, at a time. Before it was knocked down the range of buildings housed a large store, offices and workshops and squads of linesmen, jointers, electrical fitters and labourers were based there. Their region of responsibility included Montrose, Brechin, Forfar, Arbroath, Friockheim, Carnoustie and all the associated landward area. In 1969 everything was flitted to purpose-built accommodation at Elliot Industrial Estate.

Completed in just over three weeks from the day demolition of old properties began, one of Arbroath's biggest car parks, that between High Street and Hill Street, was opened on Thursday, April 6, 1967. Our picture shows a deputation of Town Councillors and burgh officials inspecting the new facility. They are, from left - Inspector James McLeod, Mr Harry Nicoll, town chamberlain; Mr George H. Rodger, burgh engineer; Mr William Samson, burgh architect; Provost R.R. Spink, Councillor Andrew Gerrard, Senior Bailie Frank W.A. Thornton and Mr Robert Robertson, town clerk.

Arbroath Abbey Theatre Club's production of Benn W. Levy's comedy, 'The Rape of the Belt', which was presented in the little theatre in May, 1967, was a sell-out even before it opened. In this vignette from the show are, from left - George S. Shepherd, Patricia Berry, Retta Robertson, Anne Cant, Helen Harvey and Alastair Duncan.

Work began at Arbroath Harbour in May, 1967, to remove a large accumulation of silt at the slipway. The £2,300 contract was won by an Edinburgh firm which utilised a crane with a scoop and a fleet of lorries to remove the mud to the burgh tip at Cairnie. The route was via Old Shorehead, Marketgate, Gravesend, Guthrie Port and Cairnie Street to avoid High Street. The work was carried out as an emergency measure as a dredger was not available until later in the year and difficulty had been experienced by the boatbuilders in using the cradles on which boats were taken up the slipway for repair. The view has not changed greatly, although the block of council houses has long been demolished and the ground taken over by the boatyard.

Arbroath High School's best - head boy and girl, their deputes and the prefects - pictured at the start of the 1967/68 term. They are from left, back row - Ian Clark, Fraser MacKenzie, Colin MacDougal, Alan Connelly, Walter Ruark, Leslie Short, Arthur Simpson, Alasdair McNaughton and Alistair Marcol: middle row - Maureen Booth, Clive Hamilton-Wood, Lorna Petrie, Ruth Garden, Doreen Jessiman, Olive Clark, Alison McKechnie, Ann Berry, Edna Ewan, Myra Stuart, Elizabeth Allan, Euan Kerr, Marjory Clark, John McCann and Sheila Whyte: front row - Miss Nancy Cant, David Greig, Marjory Irvine, head girl; Mr R.G. Hay, rector; Gavin Wilkie, head boy; Anne Nicoll and Mr W.F. Ritchie.

This group of youngsters comprised class 3D At Arbroath Academy during session 1967/68. They are, from left, back row - Bill Thomson, Alistair Bennett, Ray Cargill, Jim Watt, Alan Nicol, Graham Russell, Jim Whyte and Sandy Cumming: second row - Christopher Millar, Jeffrey Wiltosz, Norman Jackson, Steven Saunders, Ed McPherson, Graham Teviotdale, Colin Cromar, John Smith and Christopher Wren: third row - Murray Lockhart, Linda Jarret, Lorna Davidson, Helena -----, Sandra Smith, Sandra Wallace, Margaret Clark, Linda Gray, Georgina McCallum, Wilma Soutar and Ian Ball: front row - Brenda Welsh, Janet Roberts, Anne Bridges, Norma Hendry, Marlyn Shaw, Erica Birse, Margaret Stewart, Marianne Addy and Sylvia Robb.

2422 (Arbroath) Squadron of the Air Training Corps has always had a strong sporting tradition and this group of cadets from March, 1967, comprises the football team which had beaten their Perth Squadron and Dunfermline Squadron opponents by 3-2 and 5-1 respectively to win through to the Scottish semi-final of the annual ATC Tournament. Pictured at the Hayshead Road headquarters are, from left, back - George Penman, Neil Forsyth, Fraser Balharry, Alan Kirkman, Ian Ball and Steven Millar: front - John Penman, Grant Reaney, Colin Spink, John Christison, George Stewart, Peter Johns and Tom Flett.

Arbroath High School primary one pupils in 1967. They are, from left, back row - Alison Will, Allan Saunders, Fiona Mathieson, Norman Sharp, Julie Lessiter, Colin Wight, Avril Shepherd, Fraser Gemmell, Caroline Simpson, David Walker and Lorna Smith; third row - Bobby Clark, Katherine Black, --------, Margaret Dye, Peter Firth, Jackie Miller, Graham Crockatt, Carolyn Miller, Timothy Lessiter, Frances Freeman and Derek Nicoll; second row - Kevin Thomson, Denise Smith, Stevie Anderson, Jacqueline Pease, Kevin Paton, Jennifer Robertson, Graeme Hogg, Jane Menmuir, Derek Stormont and Valerie Greenhill; front row - David McKenzie, Bryan Morris, Ian Strachan, Lloyd Mitchell and David Mackay.

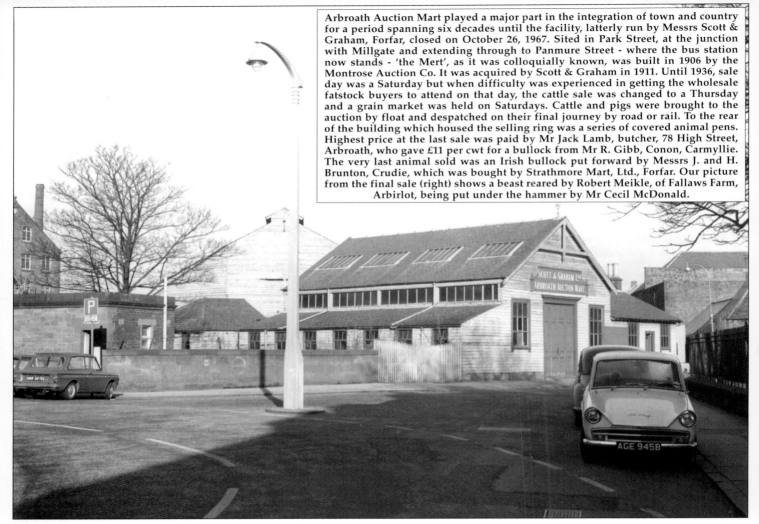

Arbroath Auction Mart played a major part in the integration of town and country for a period spanning six decades until the facility, latterly run by Messrs Scott & Graham, Forfar, closed on October 26, 1967. Sited in Park Street, at the junction with Millgate and extending through to Panmure Street - where the bus station now stands - 'the Mert', as it was colloquially known, was built in 1906 by the Montrose Auction Co. It was acquired by Scott & Graham in 1911. Until 1936, sale day was a Saturday but when difficulty was experienced in getting the wholesale fatstock buyers to attend on that day, the cattle sale was changed to a Thursday and a grain market was held on Saturdays. Cattle and pigs were brought to the auction by float and despatched on their final journey by road or rail. To the rear of the building which housed the selling ring was a series of covered animal pens. Highest price at the last sale was paid by Mr Jack Lamb, butcher, 78 High Street, Arbroath, who gave £11 per cwt for a bullock from Mr R. Gibb, Conon, Carmyllie. The very last animal sold was an Irish bullock put forward by Messrs J. and H. Brunton, Crudie, which was bought by Strathmore Mart, Ltd., Forfar. Our picture from the final sale (right) shows a beast reared by Robert Meikle, of Fallaws Farm, Arbirlot, being put under the hammer by Mr Cecil McDonald.

Members of Arbroath Round Table with wives and guests at their Christmas party in the Cafe Moderne, High Street, in 1967. Pictured are, from left - John Forsyth, Margaret Macdonald, Dave Beattie, Isobel Ramsay, George Ramsay, Joyce Jamieson, Alex Black, David Jamieson, Amy Harrison, Alex Harrison, Catherine Waggott, Jim Waggott, Peter Black, Barry Patterson and John Macdonald.

This Arbroath industrial scene from February, 1968, featuring towering sandstone and brick buildings was taken during the demolition of warehouses and workshops of Keith Blackman Ltd., fan engineers and manufacturers. The viewpoint is the junction of Applegate and Gravesend - roughly where the delivery access to Abbeygate is now - looking towards Market Place.

Principals in Arbroath Amateur Operatic Society's production of Noel Coward's 'Bitter Sweet' in the Webster Hall in February, 1968. They are, from left, standing - Alison Will, George Rodger, Edna Nicoll, John Henderson, Maureen Stormont, Margaret Hutchinson, Grace Allan, Graeme Murray, Ray Will, Patricia Murray and Jack Laing: seated - Elaine Seroczynska, Edwina Gillespie, Helen McDonald and Allan Caird.

Page 114

In appreciation of the hospitality they had received in Arbroath the previous year, ten American distributors of Giddings & Lewis Inc, Fond Du Lac, the parent company of Giddings & Lewis-Fraser Ltd, in April, 1968, presented a bust cast in copper of the late President John F. Kennedy to the town. The distributors and their wives had been given a civic reception in Arbroath Abbey. Our picture of the handover in Hotel Seaforth shows, from left - Mr Robert Robertson, town clerk; Bailie Frank W.A. Thornton, Provost R.R. Spink, Lieutenant-Colonel C.N. Thomson, chairman of Giddings & Lewis-Fraser Ltd; Mr William Somerville, managing director; and Mr J.D. (Pat) Gailey, sales manager.

In May, 1968, the Scottish National Party made its first assault on municipal politics in Arbroath, putting forward four candidates for election to the Town Council. In a clean sweep, they took two seats from Independents and two from the Ratepayers' and Electors' Association. Defeated candidates were David Goodwillie and J. Robertson, in Central Ward, and Joe Riley in East Ward. The other East Ward councillor, Mr Alex Crawford had decided not to seek re-election. Our picture shows the victorious SNP councillors who are, standing - Rev. William Scollay, Adam Simpson, Jim McGugan and William Forbes; with, seated - Mrs Scollay, Mrs Simpson and Mrs Forbes.

After 30 hours of torrential rain in May, 1968, the Brothock Burn was at its highest flood for many years. Our picture shows the scene at the old auction mart where the burn ran through the courts and along Park Street for a time.

On May 24, 1968, members of Hayshead Youth Club took to the stage in Hayshead Primary School for a concert in aid of their annual community service project. The sum of £30 was realised. The entertainers in the picture are, from left, back - Andrew Baird, Leonard Gregory, Conway Edwards, Maureen Lafferty, Heather McKenzie, Sandra McKenzie, Ian Fairweather and Brian Smith: front - Linda Pyke, Mary Shepherd, Kathleen Smith, Maureen Rennie and Marie-Anne Edwards.

Page 118

This rather grim-faced group of youngsters made up the Inverbrothock Primary School football team which contested the final of the Watters Cup competition against their counterparts from Hayshead Primary School at Gayfield Park in June, 1968. They might have been a little happier following the match, which ended in a 1-1 draw, so consequently the trophy was shared, each school having it on display for six months. Making up the team were, from left, back - Ronald Brown, David Fairweather, Keith Greenhowe, Martin Stewart, Charles Shepherd and Ian Hall: front - Alastair Forsyth, Derek Moffat, Glen Buick, Eddie Cargill, Scott Arbuthnott, Brian Longmuir and George Martin.

Principals in Arbroath High School's presentation of the Gilbert & Sullivan classic, 'Pirates of Penzance' in the Webster Hall in March, 1968. They are, from left, back - Jim Nangle, Kenneth Birse and Bill Maddox: front - Marjorie Clark, Charles Johnston, Yvonne Smith, Ruth Garden, Alison Will, Dave Cargill and Ann Verth. The show was produced by Mr J.A.R. Fraser and musical direction was by Mr B. Mordecai.

In July, 1968, television personality and wrestler, George Kidd, performed the opening ceremony at the children's paddling pool at Springfield Park, behind the fire station. The facility was the gift of Arbroath Round Table, whose members had paid for and worked on the building of the pool. Mr Kidd took off his shoes and socks, rolled up his trousers and took the first paddle, accompanied by Graham Mitchell, 1a Viewfield Road. The ceremony was chaired by Councillor Bill Millar, parks committee convener, who accepted the pool on behalf of the Town Council from Mr Stuart Ferguson, Round Table chairman. Our picture shows some of the mums, dads and youngsters who had come along for the occasion.

Representatives of the Angus Black and White Minstrels in October, 1968, visited a new school at Corseford, near Johnston, Renfrewshire, built by the Scottish Council for the Care of Spastics, where they had endowed a dormitory. During the visit, Miss Joan Mitchell handed over a cheque for £1,000 to the chairman of the council, Mr C. Laird. In the picture are, from left - Mr Laird, Mrs Amy Laidlaw, bursar; Viscount Muirshiel, who performed the opening ceremony; Mrs Jess Mitchell, Miss Joan Mitchell, Mr Norman Buchan, MP, Under Secretary of State; Mrs Maggie Hutchinson, Mr George S. Shepherd, Mrs Ivy Young and Mr Harry Will.

Eighty of the new 5p pieces were included in the ingredients of the giant Christmas pudding at HMS Condor in 1968. The traditional 'stirring' ceremony was held in the main galley during the second week in October when Captain J.W. Mott, commanding officer, Mrs Mott and Mrs Frank Bromilow, wife of the executive officer, are seen helping. Captain and Mrs Mott had a very important task, adding the rum ration to the pudding mixture.

Over the years, many local Territorials have given their lives in the service of their country and this fact is remembered annually when serving personnel take part in the Remembrance Service and parade at the war memorial. This picture, from November, 1968, shows officers and men of Q Battery, 276 Field Regiment, Royal Artillery (Volunteers) at the High Common. In front, the officers are, from left - Officer Cadet Gordon Johnstone, Lieutenant Niall Pattullo, Captain Lyndon Bolton and 2nd Lieutenant Inglis Goodfellow. The gunners and NCOs whose faces are visible include Dave Rennie, Alex Stewart, Bill Cadger, Roy Fitchett, George Ritchie, Bill Tindall, Lindsay Taylor, Ray Walker, Jock Adams, Bill White and Jock Russell.

Arbroath shoppers queued on Tuesday, October 29, 1968, for the opening of the town's latest supermarket, Coopers Fine Fare, at 195-197 High Street. First customer, Mrs Taylor, 30 Abbotsford Road, was presented with a leather wheeled shopping trolley by the store manager, Mr G. Lawson. Our picture shows shoppers about to enter the premises after the initial rush had died down.

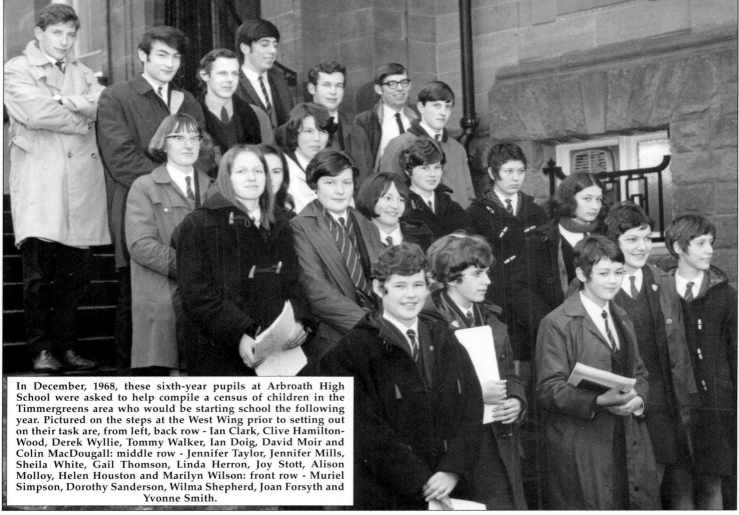

In December, 1968, these sixth-year pupils at Arbroath High School were asked to help compile a census of children in the Timmergreens area who would be starting school the following year. Pictured on the steps at the West Wing prior to setting out on their task are, from left, back row - Ian Clark, Clive Hamilton-Wood, Derek Wyllie, Tommy Walker, Ian Doig, David Moir and Colin MacDougall: middle row - Jennifer Taylor, Jennifer Mills, Sheila White, Gail Thomson, Linda Herron, Joy Stott, Alison Molloy, Helen Houston and Marilyn Wilson: front row - Muriel Simpson, Dorothy Sanderson, Wilma Shepherd, Joan Forsyth and Yvonne Smith.

Arbroath Town Councillor Mrs Ella Cargill, as convener of the Baths Committee, in January, 1969, presented medals and certificates of the Royal Life-Saving Society at a ceremony in the Hayshead Road headquarters of 2422 (Arbroath) Squadron, Air Training Corps. Our picture, taken at the event just over 25 years ago, shows some of those who received awards. They are, from left, back - Tony Smith, Brian Lancaster, Bill Dorward, baths staff; Ed Smith, Colin Watson, Ross Cargill, Brian Dickson, Eddie Marnie, Colin Spink, Tom Cameron, Ian Phillips, Jim (Peem) Moore, baths staff; Clive Hamilton-Wood, Linda Vannet, Sonia Mackay, Jeanette Brown and Tom Flett: front - Cynthia Biesok, Jane Smith, Jennifer Petrie, Janice Davidson, Ruth Eaton, Glynnis Rowlands, Ruth Dawson, Irene Hutton, Isabel McGregor and Irene Mollison.

Members of the Angus Black and White Minstrels who entertained at a cheese and wine party in February, 1969, to raise money for the British Sailors Society Ladies' Guild (Arbroath branch). In our picture, taken at Hotel Seaforth, are, from left, back row - John Henderson, Jack Laing, Charlie Brown, Joe Duncan, Douglas Cant, Jim Hutcheon, Jamie Hutchinson, Kenneth Powrie and Campbell Wilbourn; middle row - Joan Henderson, Joan Mitchell, Nan McLeod, Marlene Kear and Helen McDonald; front row - Pat Hutchison, Sheena Glover, Margaret Hutchinson, Nita Craig and Betty Lowdon. John Henderson was compere, and the singers were led by Ruth Powrie.

In March, 1969, the guest soloist with Miss Gordon's Ladies' Choir at their annual concert in the Old Church hall was baritone, John Kitchiner. George S. Shepherd was in the chair and the accompanists were Annie Doig Winter and Marion Milne. Pictured on the evening are, from left, back row - Elinor Harvey, Sheila McPherson, Joan Harvey, Isobel Fairweather, Ann Christie, Anna Duncan and Joyce Rae: second row - Jeanette Geddes, May Pankhurst, Peggy Kyle, Janie Freeland, Marion Langlands, Loris Cargill, Jennifer Deans, June Swankie, Lily Robertson, Pat Macfarlane, Lesley Pert, Mary Downie, --------, Francis Brownlie, Maureen Morrison, Maureen Crighton, Janice Norrie, May Teggarty and Mary Fallon: front row - Jean Addison, Annie Doig Winter, Mr Kitchiner, Elizabeth Gordon, Mr Shepherd, Marion Milne and Sheila McIntosh.

On Friday, April 25, 1969 Mr Ian D. Petrie, 19 Dalhousie Place, Arbroath, was licensed for the ministry at a ceremony in St Columba's Church. He was the first probationer to be licensed by the Angus and Mearns Presbytery, the first minister from the congregation of St Columba's and, as far as can be ascertained, the first in the history of the united congregations of Prince's Street and Erskine. Pictured in St Columba's Church following the ceremony are, from left - the Rev. Kenneth MacMillan, St Columba's; Rev. Gavin D. Brownlie, Ladyloan Church; Mr Petrie, Mr Alexander Petrie, session clerk; Rev. Murray Diack, Moderator of the Angus and Mearns Presbytery; and Rev. William Burns, clerk to the Presbytery.

The Hayshead Primary School team which won the Watters Cup at Gayfield Park in May, 1969, beating Carnoustie School 6-2 in the match organised by Arbroath and District Primary Schools' Sport Association. The players are, from left, back - Graham Bruce, Garry Mitchell, Ron Bowick, Ray Hardie, Grant Davidson and Colin Robertson: front - Dave Spink, Jim Tosh, Jacky Hatton, Ian Middleton and Derek McNulty.

In May, 1969, work began on the refurbishment of the Webster Memorial Hall, when workmen moved in to strip-down the interior. Within a few hours, only the main walls were left standing. Our picture provides a last glimpse of the 100-year-old hall as it was. On October, 28, 1970, the hall, renamed the Webster Theatre, was officially opened by HRH The Princess Margaret. To commemorate the occasion a plaque was unveiled in the foyer of the Theatre, and a performance of 'Martha' by Scottish Opera followed. Her Royal Highness was accompanied by Lord Dalhousie, Provost R.R. Spink and Mr Robert Robertson, town clerk.

Miss Winifred Thornton, a partner in the family firm of Messrs D. Thornton & Son, outfitters, High Street, was presented with gifts from the staff on the occasion of her retiral at a party in the Monkbarns Hotel in May, 1969. Taken on that occasion, our picture shows, from left, back - Miss Teviotdale, Joyce Thornton, May Cook, Carol Hurst, Elsie Rogers, Barbara Clark, Edna Duff, Irene Milne, Rosemary Jarret, Nan McCrodden, Mona Thomson and Ella Smith: front - Jean Thornton, Miss Thornton and Laura Brown.

The Lads' Club under-16 team which in season 1969/70 won the Maclay Cup and the League Shield. The players are, from left, back - Alan Nelson, Nairn Kerr, Ian Munro, George Reid, John Clark and Bruce Nicoll: front - Kenny Graham, Stewart Marnie, Scott Gillespie, captain; Brian Johnson and John Martin.

In June, 1969, Linda Vannet, a member of the 12th Arbroath Company, Girl Guides, was presented with the Queen's Badge by former District Commissioner, Mrs Jean Fraser, in the Guide Headquarters, Ogilvy Place. The girls looking on are, from left - --------, Glenda Jack, Jennifer Milne, Barbara Rennie, Heather Hepburn, Morag Aikman, --------, Mary Spink, Arlene Ingram, Sandra Cargill, --------, Frances Cuthill, Sheena Lakie, Anne Vannet, Lynne Martin, Joyce Booker, Marion Vannet, Jacqueline -----, Gaye Davidson, Joyce Milne, Aileen Esplin, Linda Ingram, --------, Heather Mill and Helen Bowman.

Teenage members of St Columba's Church Badminton Club who presented a highly original concert in the church hall on June 16/17, 1969. Musical direction was in the hands of Jimmy Robertson, with Valerie Jeffrey as accompanist. Our picture shows the company in the finale with, from left, back - Ruth Beattie, Fraser Mackenzie, Fiona Urquhart, Margaret Lockhart, Sheena MacDougall, Sylvia Stephen and Lynne Macdonald; front - Peter White, Jeanette Lawes, George Cant, Anne Christie and Murray Lockhart. The sailors, with heads bowed at the back of the picture, included James Nangle, Walter Ruark and Neil Ritchie. Also taking part were guest performers, Robin Fairweather, Alex Winton and George Ramsay as three mournful, black-draped, banner-carrying 'Latter Day' forecasters on a mountain top, in a sketch written by Elizabeth Allan. The Rev. Kenneth Macmillan was compere.

The Bell Rock fish restaurant, Ladyloan, run by the late Mr Greg Mandla, as it appeared in 1969 at the time it was vacated prior to being knocked down to make way for the inner relief road. The premises were acquired by Mr Mandla in 1951 and his business thrived, particularly during the summer months when there was a huge influx of holidaymakers to the town, and also at weekends, when midnight bathers would stop off for chips on the way home, or caravanners required a snack on the way back to the Red Lion site from the town. However, in the late 1960s, Arbroath's town planners came up with the idea of an internal relief road and the premises were acquired through a compulsory purchase order. Mr Mandla then moved to a purpose-built facility on the other side of the road which he named the Vandona restaurant, after his daughters, Vanda, who was involved in the family businesses and who died in 1989, and Dona.

The Arbroath High School primary football team of season 1969/70 pictured at Ogilvie Park. The players are, from left, back - Martin Brownlie, Hamish Fairweather, Malcolm Gray, Ewan Rae, Fraser Tunstall, Ian Gerrard and Brian Bush: front - Ronnie Edward, Hugh Cowan, Ernie Whyte, Robin Brunton and Malcolm Edwards.

This aerial picture of Arbroath was taken at the end of the 1960s and highlights the huge changes which have been wrought in the town since that time in the name of progress. In the foreground, the harbour is bustling and alive with numerous vessels berthed in both the inner and outer areas, at the oiling quay and beached on the slipway next to the lifeboat shed. To the left is the grainstore, a huge wooden building which did not survive much beyond the time the picture was taken. At the time, traffic still used Ladyloan and Shore to gain access to the town from the south. To the right of the outer harbour, adjacent to the municipal slipway, is a block of council houses which is no more. In the middle distance, the huge works of Keith Blackman Ltd, fan engineers, Giddings and Lewis-Fraser Ltd, engineers, and Francis Webster & Sons, flax manufacturers, are prominent. The large car parks at the bottom of High Street have not yet been built, not have the huge housing estates along the heights on either side of the Brothock valley beyond Wardmill Dam. The cluster of white buildings on the outskirts of the town in the centre of the picture is the group of prefabs which made up Cairnie Crescent.

Brothock Bank House, the charming Victorian sandstone building which housed the offices of Messrs Clark, Oliver, Dewar and Webster, solicitors, and the local branch of the National Commercial Bank. Latterly, until the building was demolished in 1969 to make way for the dual-carriageway through the town, one side of the ground floor was occupied by John Chisholm, Arbroath's publicity officer, and his staff, and the other was leased by Arbroath Amateur Boxing Club and used as a gymnasium and training centre.

All the pictures in this publication are available to purchase as 10" x 7" prints presented in an attractive folder. The black and white pictures cost £5 and the colour pictures on the cover are £7.95.

For customers living away from Arbroath, we will be pleased to send orders by post for an addition fee of £1.20 for UK orders, and £2.50 for those to be posted abroad.

Please fill in the form below, making sure to provide a complete address with postcode. Alternatively, you may write to us making sure to enclose all the information.

Picture or pictures required (page number[s]) and number of copies (i.e. x2)

....

Total remittance enclosed...

Name...

Address..

....

....**Postcode or Zip**...

Send your order to -

**Arbroath Herald,
1960s Bookie,
Burnside Drive, Arbroath, Angus,
Scotland,
DD11 1NS.**